Mohammad-Munir Adi

The Usage of Social Media in the Arab Spring

Internet Economics
Internetökonomie

edited by
herausgegeben von

Prof. Dr. Julia Maintz
(Cologne Business School (CBS) –
European University of Applied Sciences)

Volume / Band 8

LIT

Mohammad-Munir Adi

The Usage of Social Media in the Arab Spring

The Potential of Media to Change Political Landscapes throughout the Middle East and Africa

LIT

This book is printed on acid-free paper.

Bibliographic information published by the Deutsche Nationalbibliothek
The Deutsche Nationalbibliothek lists this publication in the Deutsche Nationalbibliografie; detailed bibliographic data are available in the Internet at http://dnb.d-nb.de.

ISBN 978-3-643-90468-3

A catalogue record for this book is available from the British Library

Klosbachstr. 107
CH-8032 Zürich
Tel. +41 (0) 44-251 75 05
Fax +41 (0) 44-251 75 06
E-Mail: zuerich@lit-verlag.ch
http://www.lit-verlag.ch

LIT VERLAG Dr. W. Hopf
Berlin 2014
Fresnostr. 2
D-48159 Münster
Tel. +49 (0) 2 51-62 03 20
Fax +49 (0) 2 51-23 19 72
E-Mail: lit@lit-verlag.de
http://www.lit-verlag.de

Distribution:
In Germany: LIT Verlag Fresnostr. 2, D-48159 Münster
Tel. +49 (0) 2 51-620 32 22, Fax +49 (0) 2 51-922 60 99, E-mail: vertrieb@lit-verlag.de

In Austria: Medienlogistik Pichler-ÖBZ, e-mail: mlo@medien-logistik.at
In the UK: Global Book Marketing, e-mail: mo@centralbooks.com
In North America: International Specialized Book Services, e-mail: orders@isbs.com
e-books are available at www.litwebshop.de

This book is dedicated to all those who have **fallen** during the Arab Spring and to those who are still fighting for democracy and basic human rights.

Table of Contents

TABLES

FIGURES

PREFACE

In the following research, Mohammad-Munir Adi analyzes the integration of the Internet and social media platforms in the recent political movements in the Middle East and Africa which became known as 'Arab Spring'. The paper documents that a mutual reinforcement of growing Internet connectivity and usage of social media platforms on the one side and an increasing awareness of digital tools as means for political organization and mobilization on the other side has taken place in the context of the Arab democratization movements. It shows how different platforms of the diversifying social media landscapes -- such as (micro)blogs, social networking, video sharing, and voice over IP sites including Twitter, Facebook, YouTube and Skype -- have been used as information channels and tools for political activism, including by key individuals who developed to leading figures in the revolutionary movements. Moreover, the paper sheds light on counter approaches of the challenged regimes, which reacted by blocking Internet access, Internet surveillance, and the manipulation of contents. The paper reports the combination of physical and digital strategies on both sides, the side of the protesters and the side of the questioned regimes, and highlights the international contextualization of events.

The present research realizes an important documentation of digital activism, including citizen journalism, and information warfare in the context of the Arab Spring.

Cologne, 08 December 2013
Prof. Dr. Julia Maintz, Cologne Business School

ACKNOWLEDGMENT

I am incredibly grateful to my advisors Prof. Michael Schwertel and Prof. Dr. Julia Maintz, who have assisted me in so many ways along the way.

Furthermore I am grateful for the support from my sister Karima, who has always been the one person to do it all: she advised, reviewed, inspired, motivated and always offered constructive criticism.

A special thank you to Kate, Ali, Lina, Yllzon and Sead, who patiently read through this paper over and over again.

Last but not least, I would like to thank my grandfather, Prof. Dr. M. Mamoun Hariri, my parents and the rest of the family for supporting and believing in me.

1 Introduction

In the upcoming paper, I will focus on the use of different social media platforms in the Middle East and North Africa, in order to elaborate on the potential of the media to change political landscapes. The question has been repeatedly raised whether the uprisings can be linked to the growing activities on different social media platforms and what influence increasing Internet penetration might have had and continues to have on the process during times of war. In this paper, I will analyze the role social media plays for both the insurgents and the government, the potential effects it has on international policy and whether or not the revolutions could have taken place without the use of social media.

This topic is of great importance, due to its current relevance to global politics, globalization and an ever-changing media landscape. Most of the uprisings have ended and some have brought about the fall of regimes. Others, like in Syria, have been going on for over two years. These facts have led me to take interest in the differences in the political scenes and backgrounds, the circumstances that lead to the revolts and particularly in the role of media in the Arab world's transformation process.

This paper is divided in several chapters which deal with different aspects concerning the events. At first I give insight into the political landscapes across the Arab countries, continuing with the political and socio-economic background of countries throughout the region. Next, I will review the role of new media and its importance during the Arab Spring, followed by how online activism can lead to offline protest. I will then shed light on the different media systems in Tunisia, Egypt and Syria. I proceed by analyzing the social media landscape in examining the usage of Facebook, Twitter and other relevant platforms. By establishing this basis, I give examples of individuals who play a major role in cyber activity and the government's engagement for other purposes. I will then discuss the importance of traditional media and its adaptation to the newest technology. In the last part, I will describe the role of Al-Jazeera, ending the chapter by giving particular examples for undercover journalism. Last but not least, I will end the paper with a conclusion that includes findings and compiles the answers to the questions raised in the beginning of the research.

2 METHODOLOGY

In the following chapter, I will explain the approach used to tackle the formulated research question, providing details on how I gathered information that serves to point out the reliability of the content.

I expect to find clear differences between the countries‘ political and media environments. Furthermore, I am certain that the role of social media will be even clearer, using statistics (*i.e.,* Arab Social Media Report by the Dubai School of Government, Knowledge Report, *etc.*) to prove its influence on the different uprisings. Furthermore, I hope that my analysis will help to understand the complex nature of this crisis. Revealing this complexity and putting it into words is a result I long for.

With the help of several online and offline libraries (*ub.uni-koeln.de, search.ebscohost.com*, *kug.ub.uni-koeln.de*), finding suitable journals and books over the Internet is unproblematic. Due to the currentness and the permanently evolving events, few academic works have been published. Certain experts on Arab politics have nevertheless written about these events, mostly focusing on the concluded occurrences in Tunisia, Libya or Egypt. Renowned Middle Eastern experts, like Marc Lynch or Hamid Dabashi, have published literature dealing with the Arab uprisings, which will be of great use for the thesis. Another relevant work seems to be the book containing symposium proceedings of the Deutsche Welle Media Dialogue which was held in May 2012. Several authors (*i.e.,* Christoph Schmidt, Asiem El Difraoui and Mohammad Ayish, *etc.*) have contributed to their findings concerning the protest movements.

Many journals (*i.e.,* Heinrich Böll Stiftung - Perspectives Journal) publish electronic articles that can be downloaded and used for free. Other useful sources are newspaper articles published online (*the Guardian, New York Times, Al-Jazeera, Syria Comment, Wall Street Journal, BBC News, etc.*).

Analyzing the usage of social media during the Arab Spring and examining in how far media has the potential to change political landscapes is the main goal of this paper. Whether or not media supported the revolutions in one way or the other will be verified by the used literature.

3 THE ARAB SPRING

The Arab Spring describes the continuous revolutionary movement in the Arab world. The waves of demonstrations were sparked by the actions of one man: the Tunisian fruit seller Mohamed Bouazizi who lit himself on fire as a sign of protest against police brutality in Tunisia on the 17th December 2010 (Blight, Pulham & Torpey, 2011). Ultimately, the young man died 18 days later and caused a nation wide appeal to demonstrate against the violent approach of the police and the common discontent about unemployment (Hill, 2013, p. 7). Today, this incident is often described as the trigger for an unforeseeable chain reaction in several Arab countries. However, this is just one factor in a larger fraction.

The developments in Egypt and Tunisia showed how the masses can succeed in bringing down the oppressing regimes after decades of fear and tyranny. Some people compare the Arab revolt with the 1848 revolutionary movement that rolled through Europe and ended with the repression of the demonstrators (Nazemroaya, 2011). Even though the outcome differs to the current events, the roots of the movement are similar: discontent with the authoritarian regime and a call for democracy, increasing poverty and unemployment, the poor economic situation and the state's corruption in governmental and business affairs (Mohamadieh, 2012, p. 114). However, in other countries like Bahrain and Jordan the demonstrators were silenced and oppressed. A revolution of such kind had been unseen in the Arab world so far. Surely one must differentiate between the countries and analyze what causes every uprising had, but the movements undoubtedly mutually sparked off one another (Atassi, 2011, p. 31).

Egypt, Libya, Tunisia, Morocco, Jordan, Bahrain, Algeria, Saudi Arabia, Yemen and Syria - currently the most prominent example - are all states, in which the revolts took different paths due to their political landscapes, the magnitude and pace of the protest, the involvement of outside parties and governments and last but not least the role traditional and especially online media had on the movements.

One universal factor that collectively vanished was the fear of speaking up and taking the protest to the streets (Kassim, 2012). Fear is one constant that held the people back from revolting against their oppressors on such a large scale years before. However, movements like these do not take place over night, they rather descend from underlying disaffection. Hill argues that in the case of Tunisia and Egypt observers were surprised by the uprisings, although in Egypt "[t]he revolution had been building for at least a decade" (2013, p. 64).

Not only governments, but also the international community at first repelled any possibility of social change in the Arab world long before the first incidents in Tunisia. Hill even goes further by saying that "[i]t is a sign of how much political and media establishments in many countries are wedded to the status quo and can't imagine a major change" (2013, p. 66). This avoidance to report about the outbursts is blamed on the channel's fear of loosing their credibility. Several weeks into the uprisings, the world's view changed, every international news agency adapted and began to report about the incidents (Hill, 2013, p. 61).

3.1 Political background

The uprisings in North Africa spread rapidly, causing severe and unexpected unrests in the Arab region. Mohamed Bouazizi torched a fire that was symbolic for the upcoming agitations in the months to come (Atassi, 2011, p. 28).

3.1.1 Tunisia and Egypt – *The Past*

The reasons for the outbreak in Tunisia are manifold (Awad, 2011, p. 126). Bouazizi protested against the nation's abusive police forces, high unemployment across the country and increasing poverty. His 'self-immolation' quickly spread over social media sites to international television broadcasters, which lead to a nation wide wave of demonstrations. According to Bouazizi's relatives, people protested with 'a rock in one hand, a cell phone in the other' (Ryan, 2011b). This quote stands for the people's effort, taking their protest to the streets and simultaneously recording the events with their mobile devices making the rest of the world watch. The Tunisian protest lasted for a month, before the army refused to engage in violent counteraction. The president Zine el-Abidine Ben Ali fled the country the next day, bringing his 23-year old rule to an end (Ryan, 2011a).

The Egyptian activists were eagerly following the successful protests in Tunisia, which were used "[...] to show the Egyptians that they could actually win [...]" preparing their own upheaval against their president Hosni Mubarak (Lynch, 2012b, p. 85). On January 25th 2011, a day of protest was called for in the name of Khaled Said, a fellow citizen, who died several months before, while being held in police custody. Wael Ghonim, a known Internet activist and former Google executive, later apprehended this incident (Lehnen, 2011, p. 93). He founded a Facebook page titled 'We are all Khaled Said' and called for the people to spread the message and collectively take their frustration to the streets. Besides other long-term reasons, this incident is often described as the catalyst of the Egyptian Revolution (Rabbani, 2011, p. 12). The protest on Tahrir square evolved and international voices began to call for the resignation of president Mubarak. Refusing to resign, the government tried to overwhelm the protesters by force and heavy clashes between pro-regime supporters and pro-democracy protesters emerged. With the help of defected military forces, the people regained control over Tahrir Square and continued their peaceful protest. Shaken from the past events, the protesters needed several days to regroup, but finally watched Egypt's vice president Omar Suleiman declare Mubarak's resignation on the 11th of February 2011 (Lynch, 2012b, pp. 96-98). This announcement led to the flooding of Tahrir Square of even more relieved citizens.. Consequently, Hamid Dabashi states: “As physical space, urban metaphor, and revolutionary allegory, Tahrir Square is central to the Egyptian - and by extension Arab uprising” (Dabashi, 2012, p. 99).

These world-shaking incidents in Tunisia and Egypt further stimulated people across the Arab nations. The Syrian Arab Republic is the counter example for a country in which the uprising has been going on for over two years and has no foreseeable end at the time of writing this paper.

3.1.2 SYRIA – *THE PRESENT*

The unrest in Syria firstly erupted on the 17th of March 2011, when security forces of the Assad government killed five protesters during a demonstration calling for reforms, in the southern city of Daraa (The Guardian, 2011). According to unconfirmed sources sporadic demonstrations had already taken place in the capital Damascus in February of 2011, before the protests of Daraa in March. The protest in the capital followed after the son of a shop-owner was allegedly beaten and arrested by a police officer in broad daylight. Different sources confirm that about 1500 civilians then decided to take their frustration to the streets of Damascus and chant for justice. Contrary to prevailing opinions, this peaceful demonstration already showed the ability of the Syrian people to assemble in an organized method (Landis, 2011).

Right from the start of the Arab Spring president Assad strictly dismissed any possibility of protests occurring in his nation and dissociated from the uprisings in Tunisia and Egypt. In a rare interview with *The Wall Street Journal* on the 31st of January 2011, Assad stated:

> Syria is stable. Why? Because you have to be very closely linked to the beliefs of the people. This is the core issue.

> When there is divergence between your policy and the people's beliefs and interests, you will have this vacuum that creates disturbance.

Not only did he reject the possibility of an uprising, but he was certain that he had enough time to gradually push for reforms and satisfy the Syrian people, of whom the majority are "[...] deeply depoliticized" (Norhausen and Schmid, 2011, p. 129, own translation). What followed are people peacefully chanting for reforms to strictly demanding a regime change. Bashar al-Assad's ignorance swiped away any chance of a peaceful and democratic transition. People now began chanting and protesting against police brutality, the prevailing emergency law, corruption and pleading for the resignation of their president (Khoury, 2011, p. 80). The regime's answer was a combination of vague reform promises and brutal use of force. The protest spread across the country, but unlike in Cairo, which instantly became the center of the uprising, the Syrian government forces succeeded to keep the capital Damascus and the economic metropolis Aleppo closed off from severe turmoil. Through roadblocks and media censorship the regime effectively prevented the various demonstrations of joining together and conquering public spaces in the capital (Asseburg, 2013, p. 12). Asseburg finally states that theoretically there are three scenarios: a negotiated transition between the regime and opposition, continuous fighting and further fragmentation of the country and the most unlikely scenario, being the fall of the regime (2013, p. 16).

3.2 Socio-Economic Background

Socio-economic developments vary from country to country and are permanently evolving. In the run-up of the uprisings, differences in economic and social factors between the more developed (Egypt, Tunisia) and the developing countries (Syria) were evident (United Nations Development Programme, 2011, pp.108-110). However, civil unrests were recorded nearly in every Arab country from North

Africa, to the Middle East and even the economically stable Gulf states. The reasons for the uprisings were a manifestation of homogenous discontent, which had grown over the last decades. The unwillingness of Arab governments to change, develop and progress over time is reflected in their inability to respond to the demands and interests of the people (Mohamadieh, 2011, p. 118).

The Arab Development Challenges Report 2011, which is annually led by the United Nations Development Programme (UNDP), states that "[i]nclusive participation of social and political institutions that mobilize and articulate collective interests [...] ultimately enhances the ability of states to defuse social conflict". However, a dozen Arab governments have failed to listen to the demands that were chanted on the streets. These demands have deeper roots and are related to the socio-economic developments and the political landscapes in the different regions.

Tunisia is the only Arab country that "[...] has achieved sustained growth since 1960 and has been able to satisfy the requirements of a structural economic transformation [...] between 1970 and 2007" (The Arab Development Challenges Report 2011, p. 108). Nevertheless, the economic growth of a country does not certify the satisfaction of its people. The former President Zine El Abidine Ben Ali was forced to flee the country, stubbornly cleaving to power and unwilling to call for reforms, neither on a political, economic or social level. At first, the revolution was triggered by Mohamed Bouazizi's call for freedom, followed by "[...] factors of economic and social exclusion and quickly built up towards mass mobilizations behind political demands" (Mohamadieh, 2011, p. 114).

Numerous socio-economic problems exist and have constantly increased over time. The reasons vary from a persistent and growing youth unemployment, reduction of nominal GDP in the developing countries, corruption and repression, unfair elections and "[...] a lack of voice and the ability to have a say and to take individual initiative in building the foundations for a better future" (Andersson and

Djeflat, 2013, p. 36). These problems have increasingly emerged in Syria, a developing country that misallocates resources, making counterproductive investments, luring foreign companies and neglecting the development of the employment sector (Matar, 2012). Furthermore, income inequality and rising poverty impaired living conditions in Syria. Matar (2012) detected that the monthly earnings of a Syrian worker roughly estimates to $274, "[...] thereby indicating that the majority of wage-earning people were hardly surviving".

A central driver for the uprising in Egypt in 2011 was the increasing poverty as well. Other central factors that seethed under the reign of former president Mubarak were poor education, high youth unemployment, corruption and repression, bad living conditions and the lack of political participation. Dr. Ibrahim Awad correctly stated that once the people realized that the lack of democracy in their country was one of the reasons "[...] for their deteriorating living conditions [...]", they started protesting for the cause (2011, p. 128). Not only since the brutal murder of the blogger Khaled Said in 2010, a steady growth of activism was recognized in Egypt. The revolutionary thoughts that firstly erupted in the neighboring country Tunisia "[...] sprouted so easily on the banks of the Nile, because it landed on fertile soil" (Rabbani, 2011, p. 12).

The GCC countries ('Gulf Cooperation Council'), namely Kuwait, Qatar, Saudi Arabia, United Arab Emirates, Bahrain and Oman, have not been spared by the uprisings either. Given the strong economic structures, the governments were able to engage "[...] in fiscal stimulus for short-term relief [...]" (Andersson and Djeflat, 2013, p. 41) and to counteract against potential threats. However, Oman and above all Bahrain were struck by heavy demonstrations, which in the case of Bahrain emerged in the discontent between two religious groups, which was antagonized by the GCC (Lynch, 2012b, p. 104). This shows that as long as fertile ground for potential crisis exists, whether of religious, economic or political nature, no nation is excluded from occurring turmoil.

The kingdom of Jordan is an example for an Arab state that managed to antagonize the emerging protests by complying with some of the protester's main demands. In the past, "[h]e [King Abdullah] had performed a shake-up of this kind many times before, but never under the pressure of the people" (Norhausen and Schmid, 2011, p. 152, own translation). Jordan has been ruled under the mission to "[...] either initiate a political process of reforms or stabilize a potentially dangerous situation" (Norhausen and Schmid, 2011, p. 159, own translation). Given the existing fertile ground, being the constant struggles between the native Transjordanians and the opposing Palestinian immigrants, the potential for civil unrest does exist (Norhausen and Schmid, 2011, p. 153). However, the active approach of the inclusive government has spared the nation a bloody civil war up until today.

4 THE ROLE AND IMPACT OF NEW MEDIA IN THE ARAB SPRING

Generally most experts dealing with the question whether social media caused or catalyzed the Arab Spring concur with the idea that online networks were used as a tool, rather than a cause (Schmidt, 2012, p. 19). However, there are some people who tend to one of two extremes, either arguing that "[...] the internet is the only explanation necessary [...]" or denying, "[...] that the presence of the internet can have made an impact at all" (Hill, 2013, p. 74). Both views are too limited and omit several complex factors. Ultimately, further research and analysis of these tools is necessary to decisively say whether or not there has been an impact.

Nevertheless, the combination of both online organization and offline protest is seen to be the most effective path in overthrowing repressive regimes (Atassi, 2011, p. 32). Yet it remains difficult to measure the significance of the impact social media had on convincing people to take their protest to the streets and triggering a 'democratic snowball' (Eid, 2011, p. 19) throughout the region. Ramesh Srinivasan (2012) also highlights two prominent views, one being that social media is seen as the tool that empowered the people to revolt and the other as it being a 'double-edged sword'. However one puts it, it is undeniable that the Internet and especially social networks have caught the attention of regimes, which lead those in charge to reconsider the role of these new mediums as well. The freedom of press and the free flow of information have been restricted ever since the emergence of repressive governments, which nowadays seek total control whether in form of online content or offline activism (Khoury, 2011, p. 81).

4.1 FROM ONLINE TO OFFLINE ACTIVISM

In times of mass media and rapid communication networks it is difficult to predict such events like the Arab Spring. Andersson and Djeflat endorse the abruptness in which the protests took their run, while acknowledging the importance of modern technology, which helped the protest to progress and flourish (2013, p. 34). Noll (2011) argues that the Internet can generate masses before they are even visible on the streets. This argument is reflected in the stagnant youth, which has been chomping at the bit for quite a while. The uprisings in Tunisia and Egypt clearly show how social media platforms can be used as an efficient instrument to mobilize the online activists, pushing them towards offline activism on the streets, where they make change happen. Consequently, El Difraoui states that "[r]evolutions and political change continue to be initiated by human beings", thereby countering a misleading "[...] technical determinism postulating that the Internet led to democratization and regime change" (2012, p. 62). This again amplifies the importance of the Internet as a tool for organizing, assembling and calling for protest, rather than being the catalyst of social change (Hill, 2013, p. 81). Furthermore, social media undoubtedly accelerated the speed at which information traveled across nations and provided the means for individuals to communicate with others across boarders (Lynch, 2012a). This universality enabled information and knowledge to spread at an unimaginable pace and circumvent any delay, reaching the people in real time and according to McLuhan (1964), transforming the world into a 'global village'. Beyond that, Hussein Amin, a professor of mass communications in Cairo states: "[s]ocial networks have broken the psychological barrier of fear by helping many to connect and share information" (Kassim, 2012). These commonalities among the various Arab citizens created a sense of unity and solidarity, reinforcing the belief in the revolutions' cause and aiding to dissolve the fear that had been growing upon the people over decades.

4.2 Restrictive media systems

According to Schmidt (2012, p. 7), "[...] social networking sites such as Facebook and Twitter [...] played a significant role in countries with severe restrictions on freedom of expression". He continues by comparing the political development with the media systems of the particular countries, stating that media has been in the hands of the governments for decades (2012, p. 14). In the case of Tunisia, Egypt and Syria there are essential differences. Schmidt depicts Tunisia's media environment, as being "[...] one of the worlds most restrictive [...]" (2012) and Reporters without Borders state, "[...] Tunisian authorities have been pervasively blocking and filtering political and social online content as well as entire websites and online tools" (Schmidt, 2012, p. 16). According to Freedom House, a non-governmental organization, Tunisia's media system has preceded to be partly free after the fall of the regime, which also applies to Egypt. With the beginning of the protests, the Egyptian government did not shut down the Internet, "[...] but instead concentrated on Internet surveillance and real-life harassment of journalists, cyber-activists, bloggers and human right activists" (Schmidt, 2012, p. 16). Egypt's former president later on chose to cling to his power and ideals by temporarily turning off the Internet, rather than further monitoring social media and understanding "[...] the genuine depth and scope of popular frustration so as to respond to it more productively, or at least by meeting some of the demands of the protesters" (Delong-Bas, 2011). The government could no longer control information, as it had done decades before. The speed at which information was spread and communication was transmitted between the people was eventually key to the success of the downfall of the regime.

This rapid success in Tunisia and Egypt motivated the Syrian people to seize the moment and protest against their regime too. In contrast to Tunisia's and Egypt's media systems, Syria is currently ranked as not free. The freedom of expression and other civil liberties are heavily restricted (Freedom House, 2013). The people in Syria access the Internet through state-run servers and many websites are blocked by the government (Freedom House, 2011). Nevertheless, the supporters of the demonstrations have managed to skirt around existing restrictions and make use of the media tools to their advantage (Baiazy, 2012, p. 21). Seemingly, these platforms have mainly been highly praised, which is true for some, but not so true for others. It showed how new mediums today can help the flow of information both within and outside the country, facilitating protest organization and convincing the people to join the protest. However, according to Marc Lynch (2013) "[t]he sectarian hatred and division fueled by the Syrian bloodshed flowed through social media just as effectively as the unifying message of the early Arab Spring". This fact clearly shows the power of images and videos that can stir up both positive and negative effects in people. Some scholars argue that the brutality of the events induced fear and obedience, so that a more rapid wave of demonstrations was prevented in an earlier stage of the protest. Lynch (2013) argues that this brutal and real material made the difference to the more peaceful revolutions in Egypt or Tunisia:

> There is something very different about scrolling through pictures and videos of unified, chanting Yemeni or Egyptian crowds demanding democratic change and waking up to a gory image of a headless 6-year-old girl on your Facebook news feed. Again, this reflected Syria's reality -- but that reality was amplified by Social Media.

Others point out that these images made people realize the gravity of the events for the first time and the necessity to protest against the regime. It is possible to argue the one way or the other. Undoubtedly, Syria's political transition process is unparalleled to any other uprising in the Arab region. One essential difference is the governments handling of the emerging importance of the Internet. El Difraoui argues that the regime in Syria has "[...] rapidly grasped the importance of Web 2.0" (2012, p. 84). Against all odds, the government has lifted the censorship of Facebook and YouTube, which were only accessible through proxy servers in the past. Internet in Syria is run by two major Internet service providers (ISP), which are the state owned Syrian Telecom and the SCS-Net, owned by the Syrian Computer Society (Oghia and Indelicato, 2010, p. 11). In total, there are about 11-14 ISPs, of which most of them are privately held and operate under the surveillance of the Syrian Telecommunications Establishment (El Sharif, 2009). This clearly shows that Internet and the telecommunications infrastructure in Syria is completely in the hands of the state. Controlling the web and making these platforms accessible enabled the government to counterattack against the opposition, spread own information and campaigns and apprehend activists who are disloyal to the regime (El Difraoui, 2012, p. 84). This approach shows that governments who recognize the threat can make use of the instruments themselves. The Internet "[...] can either become a tool of oppression or instead offer an infrastructure for creating positive change [...]" (El Difraoui, 2012, p. 84). For Syria, both these sides have unfortunately been proven to be true.

4.3 Self-Empowerment of the People

Throughout the Arab Spring, social media networks did not only serve as a communication tool for the revolting youth, but also contributed to the process of self-empowerment. According to El Difraoui (2011), a social group is formed, when people collectively meet online and sharing their views and opinions. When they then meet offline, on the streets, the process of self-empowerment and identity is further enhanced through collective experiences.

Ideally, the combination of both the online and the real life activity lead to social change, as seen in North Africa. The term of the 'prosumer', coined by Alvin Toffler in his 1980 published book 'The Third Wave' is crucial (Gerhardt, 2008, p. 1). He predicts the mergence of the role of producers and consumers. The people who were consumers in the past, also become producers by recording and publishing the events. El Difraoui also states that the "[...] division between producers and users is rapidly diminishing - the 'produser' (producer + user) has emerged" (2012, p. 62). Both the 'prosumer' and the slightly modified term of the 'produser' have the same meaning. This mergence enables a constant flow of information, which makes it difficult for authorities to track the source of origin and control the content that is being transmitted.

The sheer number of 'prosumers' who successively reported on the incidents, for example, overran the governments of Egypt and Tunisia. The protesters on the streets instantly uploaded pictures and video footage onto YouTube (Howard et. al., 2011, p. 22). The governments were powerless against the distribution of information and misjudged the lack of control they had over the new mediums and their content. El Difraoui (2012) explains that the people were able to bypass the control and censorship mechanisms, by exploiting media and denouncing state violence to the general public. These actions often followed police surveillance, detention or as seen in the case of Khaled Said, death. The cyber activists gradually protected their identity by using tools like Hotspotshield, which blocked their IP-address and made them invisible to the surveiling authorities (Hill, 2013, p. 28). This tool allowed people to commit to the protest, minimizing the danger of being caught. When the Egyptian government tried to detach and isolate the country from the global flow of information, the Internet was shut down for several days in hope of regaining control with a vengeance. By resorting to mobile phones and keeping the protest alive, the government failed to cause the hoped for blackout, which would have given them the upper hand (Nordhausen and Schmidt, 2011, p. 43). Another important aspect is mentioned by Djeflat who states that social media extended the lifespan of the revolution, through a flat hierarchy and the inability of regimes to target one central leader (2013, p. 184). The division and distribution of responsibility in organizing protests lead to broad leadership structures. The general populace, being the protesters on Tahrir Square, consisted of countless individuals who all protested for the same cause.

5 Internet penetration and the social media landscape

According to the Arab Advisors Group, the number of active Internet users in the Arab countries amounted to be between 40 - 45 million in the year 2009 (Ayish, 2012, p. 106). The Arab Knowledge Report of 2010/2011, however, estimated the number to be about 60 million Internet users (Ayish, 2012, p. 106). By 2015, Google expects an increase to a total of 100 million users (Ghannam, 2011, p. 4). The numbers presented illustrate the massive growth potential of the Arab Internet landscape. However, the fluctuation clearly shows that these numbers are mere estimations.

Emma Murphy states that the most striking point is "[...] the rate at which Internet usage is now growing: between 2000 and 2007, usage in the Middle East region had reportedly grown by 920 per cent (compared with 221.5 per cent in Europe and 117.2 per cent in North America)" (2011, p. 106). To a great extent, this growth potential is due to its "[...] technologically accomplished demographic group - its youth [...]" (Ghannam, 2011, p. 6). The Arab market is steadily headed towards a promising future, in which today's youth group consists of well-educated, middle-class citizens, who strive for freedom and democracy in every possible sphere.

5.1 The Arab blogosphere

In a 2007 published article titled 'The New Arab Conversation', Gal Beckerman analyzed the Arab blogosphere, giving an outlook to what might be expected in the following years. According to Beckerman (2007), "[o]nly 10 percent of the Arab world has Internet access, yet that is a five-fold increase from 2000". Nevertheless, this tiny fraction already used the Internet to speak up and discuss controversial issues back then. The number of blogs increased steadily.

More and more blogs appeared in Jordan, Iraq and during the Cedar Revolution in Lebanon. In more conservative countries like Egypt, bloggers were rare but "[...] equally vocal" (Beckerman, 2007). Internet surveillance of blogs was common, followed by reported arrests and detention of the bloggers. Despite of emerging criticism, using pseudonyms and staying anonymous became essential to protecting one's own identity from the potential tortures many others faced across the Middle East. Marc Lynch has also written an article titled 'Blogging the New Arab Public' in the same year, saying that "[b]logging remains an activity of a tiny elite, as only a small minority of the already microscopic fraction of Arabs who regularly use the Internet actually write or read blogs" (2007, p. 1). However, according to Lynch, some independent newspapers in Egypt (Al Masry Al Youm or Al Dustour) have cited "[...] blogs as sources for their stories, offering another indirect route for political impact" (2007, p. 5). This clearly displays an increasing approval of independent opinions published on the different blogs and their increasing political significance (Lynch, 2007, p. 29).

In Tunisia, Nawaat became the most popular platform for Tunisian dissidents, discussing politics and debating about current events (Gharbia, 2011, p. 86). According to El Difraoui, Nawaat was responsible for informing citizens about bypassing Internet censorship and protecting their online identities from exposure (2012, p. 67). Another group called Takriz, engaged in fighting Internet censorship by hacking government websites with the help of the activist movement called Anonymous (El Difraoui, 2012, p. 67).

The Arab region in total estimates a number of 35,000 blogs in 2009 and 40,000 in 2010 (Ghannam, 2011, p. 5). Beckerman (2007), similarly to Lynch, depicts the bloggers' views by stating, "[...] that revolutions almost always start with a tiny elite. But we are a long way from this revolution's doorstep". He sees the potential for change in the young elite who has found a platform to voice their frustrations and vent to a mass's fury. Lynch argues and attributes blogs the capability to "[...] be catalysts for previously unlikely political mobilization" (2007, p. 2). Whether or not blogs have an impact on people's political decision-making process demands long-term research and surveys. This is however the most effective way to determine the influence of the Arab blogosphere. As Marc Lynch states, people should not focus on the possibility that blogs might facilitate change (Hofheinz, 2011), but rather on how to "[...] explore the variety of ways in which blogs might transform the dynamics of Arab public opinion and political activism" (2007, p. 3).

5.2 FACEBOOK AND TWITTER IN THE ARAB WORLD

Social media networks have had a yet to be seen impact on the Arab uprisings. Ghannam states that "[...] the real impact won't be felt for years, maybe even a few decades, observers say, when expectations and political regimes may have changed" (2011, p. 8). Facebook, being one of the two most influential platforms besides Twitter, had generated 14 million users in April 2010 and only a year later nearly doubled the number to 27 million (Schmidt, 2012, p. 17). A 30% increase was alone recorded in the first quarter of 2011.

As seen in the graph below, the Dubai School of Government has identified the total number of Facebook users and the coinciding percentage of user penetration between January 2011 and June 2012 in their Arab Social Media Reports of 2011 and 2012.

Facebook Users	Jan 5, 2011	Apr 5, 2011	Jan 3, 2012	**End June, 2012**
in million	21.377.282	27.711.503	37.390.837	**45.194.452**

Table 1: Total number of Facebook users in the Arab World

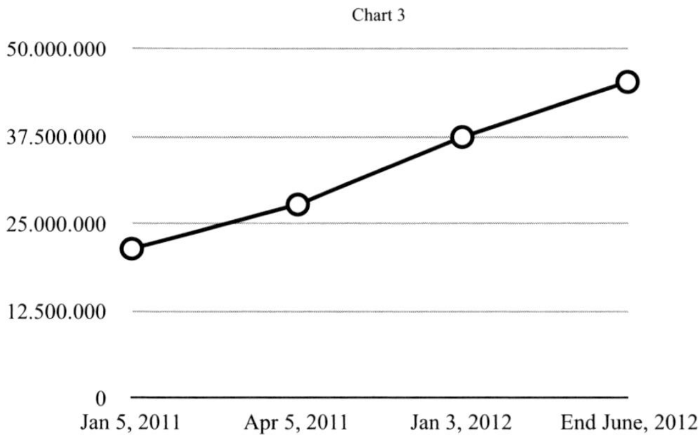

Figure 1: Total Number of Facebook users
Source: Own illustration, based on Arab Social Media Report 1/11, 5/11 and 7/12

	End of 2010	April, 2011	June, 2011	**End of June, 2012**
in percentage	6%	⬆ 7,5%	⬆ 8%	**⬆ 12%**

Table 2: User penetration

The total number of Facebook users in the Arab region reached a high of 45,194,452 million users at the end of June 2012. It is probable that the forthcoming numbers will display a further increase of active users in the region. The newest estimates count a total of 49 million Arab Facebook users in March 2013 (El Ahmad, 2013), of which youth "[...] between the ages of 15 and 29 make up 70% of the region's total Facebook users" (Schmidt, 2012, p. 17).

Twitter has also played an important role and has helped the spread of information across the globe. As the figures, taken from the Arab Social Media Reports of 2011 and 2012 by the Dubai School of Government, display, the total of Twitter users have nearly doubled in little over a year.

	active **Twitter users**		***number of*** **Tweets**	
	end of March '11	end of June '12	1/4 of '11	March '12
in million	1.150.292	⬆ **2,099,706**	22.750.000	⬆ **172,511,590**
	trending #			
	1/4 of '11		March '12	
	#egypt		#bahrain	
	#jan25		#syria *in Arabic*	
	#libya		#bahrain *in Arabic*	
	#bahrain		#syria	
	#protest		#egypt	

Table 3: Twitter Users and Tweets
Source: Own illustration, based on Arab Social Media Report 5/11 and 7/12

The most astonishing fact is, however, that the total amount of tweets has increased tremendously to amount to 172,511,590 million tweets in March 2012. Certainly the number fluctuates and hugely depends on the events during that time. The trending hashtags clearly show a shift of trending topics from one year to the other. This constantly varies according to the point in time an event is current or obsolete. In 2013, Syria is most probably the trending topic on Twitter in the region.

In Tunisia, Twitter was blocked in the four weeks of protest, yet proxies were permanently used to overcome the ban. The government also tried to constantly block the user-generated content by slowdowns and filtering methods (Comninos, 2011, p. 10). The people, however, were never cut off from the Internet, as it happened in Egypt (Ghannam, 2011, p. 16). The Egyptian government shut down the Internet on January 25th until February 2nd 2011. Internet traffic reached a low and people increasingly relied on cell phone communication and organization. The main impact of blocking social networking sites, contrary to the government's intention, was that people felt an even stronger urge to actively protest on the streets of Cairo. The Syrian regime blocked all social media platforms until February 2011 (Baiazy, 2012, p. 18). In absolute self-assertion, president Assad gave the order to lift the ban that had existed for decades. Though proxies were regularly used to avoid barriers, Internet traffic spiked after the ban was abolished (Ghannam, 2011, p. 16).

Undoubtedly, the use of Facebook helped the organization of protests, spreading the message across the borders and reaching a mass audience in all Arab countries. The platform provided "[...] a space where silence and fear are overcome and trust can be built, where social networks can turn political, and where home and diaspora can act together" (Sreberny, 2012, p. 3). Especially in repressive regimes "[...] where face-to-face public politics is extremely curtailed [...]" (Sreberny, 2012, p. 3), social media networks provided for political conversation. According to Alexa.com, Facebook is the most popular website in Egypt and Tunisia today, ranking 1st ahead of Google's search engine (Hofheinz, 2011).

The chart below shows an increase in Facebook penetration for Tunisia, Egypt and Syria. Generally, all three countries have experienced strong spikes in active Internet users and have the potential of further development.

	ASMR 1/11	ASMR 5/11
Tunisia	17,55%	⬆ 22,49%
Egypt	5,49%	⬆ 7,66%
Syria	1,07%	⬆ 1,94%

Table 4: Facebook Penetration*
Source: Own illustration, based on ASMR 1/11 and 5/11
*calculation: number of Facebook users / by the country population

However, in the case of Syria, a lot of its communication infrastructure has been destroyed. The severe use of heavy artillery over the last two years has had huge negative outcomes on the whole country. The total loss of the economy amounts to about 48.4 billion dollars and an end of the crisis is not yet in sight (Aziz, 2013).

Despite the seemingly week Facebook penetration rates, the number of Facebook users has exponentially increased from June 2010 until June 2012 according to the Arab Social Media Report website.

	June '10	Jan '11	April '11	June '11
Tunisia	**1.556.340**	1.820.880	2.356.520	2.602.640
Egypt	**3.541.720**	4.634.600	6.586.260	7.855.820
Syria	**173.499**	241.859	446.060	760.727
	Oct '11	Jan '12	June '12	
Tunisia	2.750.160	2.799.260	**2.986.700**	
Egypt	8.791.800	9.391.580	**11.000.000**	
Syria	1.369.143	1.852.566	**3.228.677**	

Table 5: Number of Facebook Users in Tunisia, Egypt and Syria

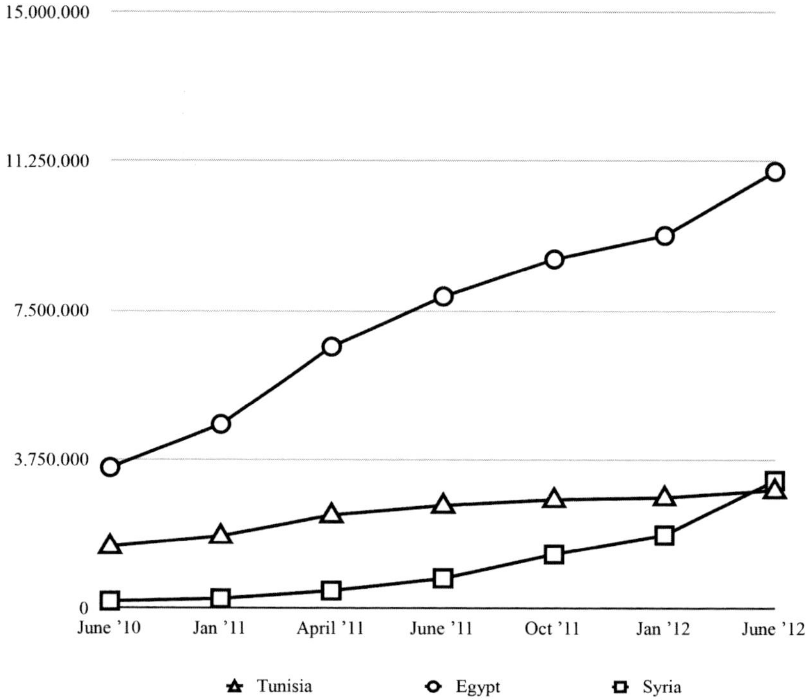

Figure 2: Number of Facebook Users in T, E & S
Source: Own illustration, based on http://www.arabsocialmediareport.com

Egypt has experienced the strongest increase, whereas Tunisia and Syria are slowly reaching higher numbers too. One must always consider the political and economical differences between these states. Syrians have been functioning in a very repressive environment, in which Internet access is very limited. Sreberny also states "Tunisians faced a more pervasive police state than the Egyptians, with less latitude for blogging or press freedom [...]" (2012, p. 4).

Twitter was used in a frequent manner as well. As Comninos states, "[n]ews coming from Twitter about events in Tunisia served to inspire people throughout the region [...]" (2011, p. 8). For Tunisians, Twitter was the prominent platform for spreading information.

The most frequent hashtags used were #sidibouzid and #Tunisia (Comninos, 2011, p. 8).

Generally, the Twitter figures contributed below show an increase in users, as well as in tweets. Though penetration is still rather low in contrast to the countries' populations, Twitter has gained increasing importance in the Arab region throughout the uprisings.
According to Howard et. al. "Twitter seems to have been a key tool in the region for raising expectations of success and coordinating strategy. Twitter also seems to have been the key media for spreading immediate news about big political changes [...]" (2011, p. 9). Despite interruptions, which were caused by Tunisian security forces, Twitter was increasingly used, with almost a thousand daily published Tweets (Howard, 2011, p. 11).

	***active* Twitter Users**		**Penetration**	
	between Jan 1 & March '11	June '12	*between* Jan 1 & March '11	June '12
Tunisia	35.746	⬇ 12,000	0,34%	0,11%
Egypt	131.204	⬆ 296,219	0,15%	0,35%
Syria	40.020	⬇ 10,839	0,17%	0,50%

	Tweets	
	between Jan 1 & March '11	*during* March '12
Tunisia	576.000	⬆ 713,000
Egypt	2.160.000	⬆ 19,530,000
Syria	783.000	⬆ 1,488,000

Table 6: Twitter, Penetration & Tweets in T, E & S
Source: Own illustration, based on Arab Social Media Report 5/11 and 7/12

Twitter was used as a tool and facilitated the communication between the people. Its increasing recognition amongst the Arab region lead the company to launch its services in the Arabic language on March 6th 2012. According to the most recent Arab Social Media Report "Arabic language is the fastest growing language ever on Twitter, among 25 other different languages used on the site" (2012, p. 2). Interestingly, the report also states that the percentage of Arabic tweets in the Arab region have instantly outdistanced English tweets (62.1% and 32.6%) in the month the Arabic Twitter interface was introduced (2012, p. 18).

5.3 YOUTUBE, SKYPE AND MOBILE PHONES

According to the Arab Social Media Report of July (Dubai School of Government, 2012, p. 23),

> YouTube playbacks doubled in the last year in the Arab region. There are 167 million video views a day in the Arab region, putting the region in the number two spot in the world (behind the U.S. and ahead of Brazil). Views in the region have grown by 120% in the last six months. One hour of YouTube video is uploaded in the Arab region per minute.

	Uploads	**Views**
	YouTube Usage 2011 vs. 2010	
Egypt	⬆ *by* 150%	⬆ 220%
Tunisia	⬆ *by* 420%	⬆ 100%
Syria	*no data available*	

Table 7: YouTube Uploads & Views
Source: Own illustration, based on Arab Social Media Report 7/12

The table shows that in both Egypt and Tunisia YouTube has increased its uploads and views exponentially. This clearly shows the importance of video platforms throughout the region and its significance as a source of information during the Arab Spring. In this case, there are no available records for Syria.

Howard et. al. (2011, p. 22) have analyzed YouTube's role in the uprisings and concluded that it helped spread viral information across the globe. This information consisted of user-generated videos that were used by both the new and old mediums. The videos mostly posted by citizens showed live footage from the streets of Tunisia, Egypt and Syria. Howard has further identified that the main types of Egyptian videos consisted of "raw protest and mobilization footage; citizen commentary; political punditry [...]" and music videos that served as soundtracks for the revolution (2012, p. 22). Aday et. al. have conducted an analysis of the role of social media in the Arab Spring as well, claiming that the "[s]hocking videos of Syrian regime forces attacking protesters, often with graphic images of the dead and wounded, seem to have powerfully shaped the global and regional response to that crisis" (2012, p. 20). The videos were uploaded on YouTube and spread over various social networking sites and mainstream media, which relied on these videos as sources due to Syria's ban of international journalists.

The event of the Arab Spring definitely contributed to the massively increasing uploads and views in the Arab countries. However, Google took the first step when the decision was made to launch YouTube in the Arab language in 2010 (Ghonim, 2010). This move secured the platform a high percentage of Arab users in the region. Microsoft Skype was actively used during the Arab Spring for communication purposes too. Especially in Syria the protesters have made use of the Voice over IP (VoIP) software. It is considered to be one of the wiretapping-resistant programs, "[...] making it safer for transmitting messages while under the watchful eyes and ears of government censors" (Fitzpatrick, 2013). It is known that the regimes have filtered, blocked and tapped the accounts of users for

Internet surveillance. Frequent Internet blackouts are induced by the Syrian regime, in order to crack down on the opponents. However, "[...] rebels have armed themselves with mobile satellite phones and dial-up modems" (Chozick, 2012) to outlive the shutdowns.

Another popular and reliable communication method is mobile phones and especially smart phones. Besides calling other participants and writing text messages, the devices were frequently used for taking pictures and recording the events on the streets (Howard et. al., 2011, p. 23). In Tunisia and Egypt cell phone use is very common. 93 out of 100 people in Tunisia are mobile phone subscribers, whereas 67 out of 100 people in Egypt actively make use of the devices (Howard et. al., 2011, p. 5).

	2000	**2001**	**2002**	**2003**	**2004**	**2005**
Tunisia	119.165	389.208	574.334	1.917.530	3.735.695	5.680.726
Egypt	1.359.900	2.793.800	4.494.700	5.797.530	7.643.060	13.629.602
Syria	30.000	200.000	400.000	1.185.000	2.346.000	2.950.000
	2006	**2007**	**2008**	**2009**	**2010**	**2011**
Tunisia	7.339.047	7.842.619	8.602.164	9.797.026	11.114.206	**12.387.656**
Egypt	18.001.106	30.093.673	41.286.662	55.352.233	70.661.005	**83.425.145**
Syria	4.675.000	6.234.682	7.056.158	10.021.861	11.799.212	**13.117.253**

Source: Own illustration, based on International Telecommunications Union (2012), Mobile-cellular subscriptions from 2000-2011

Table 8: Mobile Subscriptions in T, E & S

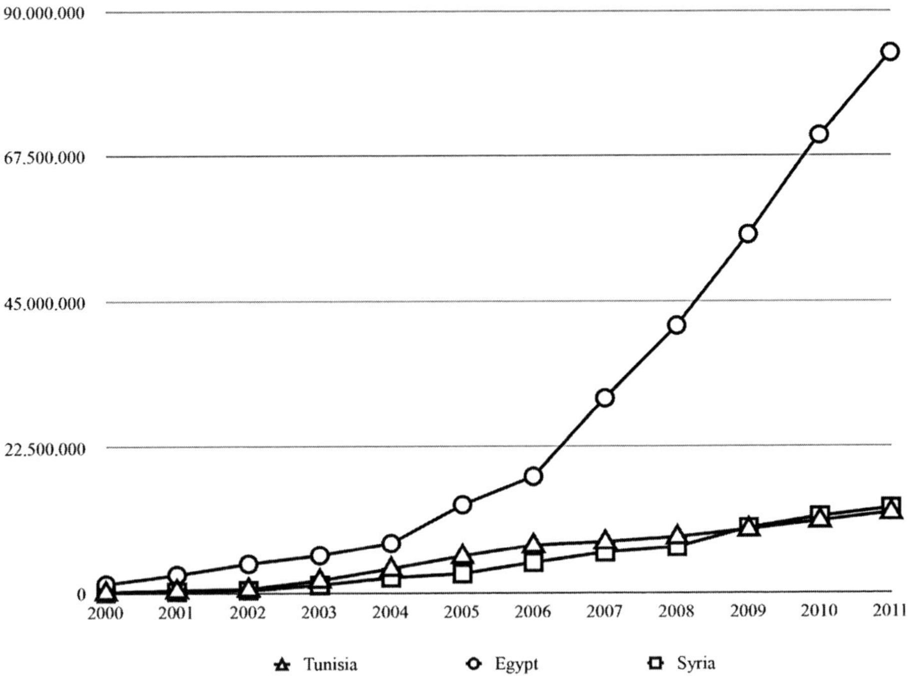

Figure 3: Mobile Telephone Subscriptions
Source: Own illustration, based on International Telecommunications Union (2012), Mobile-cellular subscriptions from 2000-2011

According to the International Telecommunications Union (2013), a vast increase in mobile phone subscriptions over the last decade was experienced in the Arab region. The graph above shows that Egypt has obtained the greatest increase of the three countries mentioned. The estimates for the year 2000 were little over a million subscribers, whereas in the year 2011, the number has mounted to 83,425,145 million cell-phone subscriptions and about 82,536,770 million inhabitants (World Bank, 2011).

However, on average 87.9 out of 100 inhabitants were owners of a subscription in the Arab region in 2010, whereas in 2005 the number was still at 27.1 subscription owners out of a 100 inhabitants (International Telecommunications Union, 2013).

Nowadays, even in a developing country like Syria, modern technology plays a great role. Especially mobile phones, which are mostly equipped with a camera and ideally an Internet connection, can be used for many purposes. As often seen on platforms like YouTube, ordinary people become field reporters, broadcasting everything they experience online. In the course of the uprising, Apples IPhone and the messaging software WhatsApp have been blocked and banned by the Syrian government (Baiazy, 2012, p. 20). As mentioned before, Syria occasionally cuts off the Internet connection, "[...] to disrupt rebel communication when regime forces are conducting major operations" (Al Jazeera, 2013). Even during blackouts the protesters try to communicate via satellite phones called Thuraya satellite phones, which are often provided by foreign entities. The company itself offers the following description on their website (http://www.ts2.pl/en/Thuraya):

> Designed to complement existing GSM networks and expand usage beyond conventional network coverage areas, Thuraya's mobile satellite services offer a broad range of services that include voice, data, fax, short messaging, GPS through its dual mode handsets.

6 THE ROLE OF CYBER ACTIVISTS

Popular movements, whether political or of any other kind, mostly have a representative who stands straight for the cause and is seen as the face of the movement. Unwillingly, Mohamed Bouazizi became that person for the people in the Arab region. However, every country needs local Avant-gardes, who drive movements forward and stimulate others to participate as well.

6.1 A TUNISIAN GIRL, SANDMONKEY & REDRAZAN

In Tunisia, the 27-year old Lina Ben Mhenni documented the uprising and became one of the most popular bloggers in the country (Ryan, 2011c). She was one of the few bloggers who reported from inside Tunisia under her real name. Unlike others, who used pseudonyms to protect their identity, she took the risk and got the attention of international media. She traveled to Sidi Bouzid, the hometown of the fruit seller Mohamed Bouazizi reporting of the incidents in the town and posting pictures from the injured protesters (Ryan, 2011c), making the extent visible to everyone.

The Egyptian blogosphere has been evolving since the year 2004. Its emergence is closely related to the political 'Kifaya movement' of the same year, which "[…] began as a petition of some 300 intellectuals in the summer of 2004, and developed an Internet presence with a popular Web site in the fall of 2004" (Lynch, 2007, p. 12). The blogging scene continued to grow over the years, until a shift to other networks like Facebook and Twitter was recognized. The last major success of bloggers during Mubarak's presidency is owed to the established Facebook group 'We are all Khaled Said' in memory of the deceased blogger (Howard et. al., 2011, p. 15). As I have mentioned before, Wael Ghonim, face of the Egyptian uprising in 2011, formed the group. Another prominent figure is Mahmoud Salem, also known under the pseudonym Sandmonkey, under which he began blogging in the year 2004. After days of detention during the uprisings in 2011, he gave up his identity (Ferran, 2011). Salem was not only a political blogger, but also an activist, involved in the protests of the democracy movement on the streets.

The Syrian female blogger Razan Ghazzawi attained prominence, being the only blogger writing in English from inside Syria. International media and Amnesty International have called her a 'prisoner of conscience' and portrayed her as being fearless in her actions. She, however, states: "I was not fearless. I am still not fearless. I wrote in English because they [the regime] don't read English. Those who are fearless are those who write in Arabic, and they write in their real name" (Malsin, 2013). Meanwhile she has fled the country for Sweden in October 2012, after being detained twice and questioned by the Syrian regime (Malsin, 2013). Her former employer, Mazen Darwish, founder of the NGO 'The Syrian Center for Media and Freedom of Expression', was arrested in 2012 alongside Razan and several other journalists (The Arabic Network for Human Rights Information, 2012). He remains detained until today. Other prominent Syrian activists, who have been detained, are Hussein Ghrer and Tal Al-Mallohi. They are considered to be the youngest detainees in Syria (Amnesty International, 2010). Shakeeb al-Jabri is another prominent blogger, who is known as @LeShaque on Twitter. He is one of the people blogging from outside the country, respectively from the Lebanese capital Beirut (Now Lebanon, 2012). In an interview with Now Lebanon (2012), a Lebanese online news website, al-Jabri admits to Syrians having the technology, but lacking the general know-how among the crowd. He too, refers to social media's crucial importance for keeping the revolution alive and the protester's dependence on organizing and reporting over the networks.

6.2 INTERNET SURVEILLANCE

Regimes have mostly neglected the importance of online platforms and underestimated the influence of Internet activists. Tunisia and Egypt are the most recent examples for governments not approaching the issue in a timely manner, thus responding with extreme measures, for instance, shutting down the Internet completely (Hoard et. al., 2011, p. 16). Bahrain and Syria, however, are counterexamples for regimes, which have actively participated in the online medium from the beginning of the protests. According to Comninos (2011, p. 10):

> Twitter and Facebook, as well as being possible instruments of protest, can also render users vulnerable to state surveillance. These platforms have been used by security and intelligence agencies to identify and locate activists and protesters (2011, p. 10).

6.2.1 TUNISIA – *BLOCKED*, EGYPT – *SHUT DOWN*

Both the Tunisian and the Egyptian government had blocked websites in the past before the uprisings in early 2011. President Zine el-Abidine Ben Ali and president Husni Mubarak at some point ordered the blockade of the social networking sites, simultaneously hoping to break down the protests on the streets (Ghannam, 2011, p. 11). Comninos states that Facebook, Twitter and several e-mail accounts were hacked and manipulated by state employees to infiltrate the activist network (2011, p. 10). Out of desperation and failure, Tunisians were then offered openly held talks to discuss demands and possible reforms (Comninos, 2011, pp. 10-11). However, by then the protesters had made up their minds about the future of the country, which did not include the president. The Egyptian government even went a step further by shutting down the Internet and in the meantime arresting and molesting individual activists. These efforts, though probably executed by highly trained personnel, lacked systematic planning. Both regimes were simply caught off guard. They then responded in ways that pushed even the last supporters over the edge of the cliff.

6.2.2 The Syrian Electronic Army

The SEA is a group of Syrian pro regime hackers, who have been monitoring and attacking the regime's opponents on the Internet since 2011. The group is believed to be hosted by the government, however, the only connection made is President Assad's praising "[...] of the Electronic Army in a June speech [...]" in 2011 (Amos, 2011). The Syrian government and its powerful intelligence agency have expanded their surveillance methods to monitor Internet communication and identify their opponents. Facebook and Twitter have officially been unlocked for the public's general use in the beginning of the uprising in February 2011, acting in absolute certainty that the protest would not escalate in Syria. Besides several Internet blackouts over the past months, which have been supposedly caused by the SEA, Internet and social media sites have been kept active until today. The latest blackout was recorded on the 8th of May 2013 and lasted for nearly two days (Al Jazeera, 2013).

The SEA has recently hacked and falsified information on Twitter's Associated Press feed (Fowler, 2013). A fake tweet, about the White House being attacked, caused a short uncertainty and fall of the Dow Jones at the stock market (Smith-Spark and Van Heerden, 2013). This incident shows the group's capabilities to hack major media outlets throughout the world. President Assad has repeatedly blamed international media for falsifying information and contributing to its distribution. The reported infiltrations at ABC News, Reuters and the Human Rights Watch (Fillion, 2013) can be seen as retaliation for the alleged accusations and "[...] demonstrate Syria's interest in disrupting the flow of information, especially the flow of information from international media" (Smith-Spark and Van Heerden, 2013). The existence of the SEA is undeniable, however, the group is entirely non-transparent. The people behind the operation are affiliated to Assad's regime, as they are posting pro-Assad propaganda (Baiazy, 2012, p. 20). Yet the location of the organization, whether inside or outside of Syria, remains unclear. Fitzpatrick argues that "[...] we may be witnessing a new global evolution in information warfare. And if it isn't, it's a sign that cyber war is quickly becoming a major component of real battles" (2013).

7 IMPORTANCE AND ROLE OF TRADITIOAL MEDIA - TELEVISION

The emerging youth, the main protagonists of the Arab Spring heavily relied on social media and the Internet during the uprisings (Nordhausen and Schmid, 2011, p. 13, own translation). Older generations that constitute to a significant mass in Arab countries mostly rely on traditional media like newspapers and television. The combination of old and new media channels connect these different generations. When Facebook groups were formed, Al-Jazeera, the Arab news broadcaster, reported on these appeals, mobilizing a generation that to some extent had never used the Internet before. The interplay between traditional and social media was necessary for the uprisings, however, not sufficient as a cause (Lynch, 2012a).

The importance of traditional media is also displayed in the case of Wael Ghonim. When he was arrested for founding the Facebook page 'We are all Khaled Said' and later released. His emotional appearance on television caused a nation wide uproar and inspired the people, who did not or rarely followed online media, to continue revolting against the regime (Deutsche Welle, 2011). In this case, Ghonim's appearance on television strengthened people's faith and further pushed Mubarak into resignation.

7.1 ADAPTATION TO THE NEW MEDIA ENVIRONMENT

Besides being a platform for organizing and calling for protest, social media was crucially important for providing information in form of video footage and pictures to international media outlets. Many news broadcasters were hesitant before making use of the material circulating on the Internet, doubting the potential of the protests at first (Hill, 2013, p. 61). Unlike most regimes, news corporations gradually understood the importance and influence of social media and made use of the material, which was sometimes difficult to authenticate (Harkin et. al., 2012, p. 10). Especially in a country like Syria, in which foreign journalists are banned from reporting from inside the country, news agencies eventually had to rely on local sources. As the war in Syria is ongoing, broadcasters still heavily depend on user-generated content and sometimes on undercover journalists, who risk their lives for generating authenticated news content (Harkin et. al., 2012, p. 6).

According to El Difraoui, "[t]he development of media into cross-media enables simultaneous, interactive, global, and multidimensional communication" (2012, p. 62). This view had to be acquired and steadily obtained by the broadcasters along the way. The separation between social media and television broadcasters like Al Jazeera or Al Arabiya is no longer possible -- not just in terms of affecting the course of uprisings, but also due to the rapid spread of information on both channels. An additional explanation is given by Khoury stating that, "[t]his is the new age of mass communication: multiple sources of information which are also conduits for change and expression" (2011, p. 84). People no longer resort to one single source, but use various old and new platforms to inform themselves about current affairs.

In times of modern technology, a shift towards new information processes has been set in motion. Through the symbiosis between the audience and the transmitter, digital conversion has not merely replaced or added content, but changed the fundamentals of television (Krüger, 2011).

7.2 THE ROLE OF AL-JAZEERA

The ruling family of Qatar founded Al-Jazeera in December 1996 in Doha, as the successor of BBC Arabic (Hofheinz, 2011, p, 2). Al-Jazeera quickly became a known institution, which reported on controversial topics that were unspoken in the Arab region. Initially Al-Jazeera was broadcasted over Arabsat (Arab Satellite Corporation) satellites, only for eight hours a day (Miles, 2005, p. 34). Today, the channel airs twenty-four hours a day and is available all over the globe. Its main viewers reside in the Middle East, however, since the English counterpart was launched in 2006, the viewership has spread all over the world. Al-Jazeera steadily developed from a regular Arab news broadcaster to a medium, which "[...] allowed the voices of the previously silent masses to be heard, challenging the communicative monopoly of the authoritarian Arab regimes in the region" (Uysal, 2011, p. 2). The format of the channel had not been seen in the region before, creating a new public open space for Arabs to discuss political and social matters.

The power of images and video footage has been demonstrated during the Arab Spring. Horrifying images and recordings of civilians being slaughtered still circulate among the news broadcasters and rapidly form the public opinion. Especially Al-Jazeera is attributed a considerable amount of responsibility concerning the influence it had on the public opinion -- although initially being cautious about reporting on the events, in fear of loosing its credibility. Even after the protests in Tunisia and Egypt, an article was published by Al-Jazeera titled 'Syria: A Kingdom of Silence', referring to Syria's seeming inability to mobilize the masses (Wikstrom, 2011).

As I have mentioned before, the development of media into cross-media, enabled Al-Jazeera to transform into an "[...] integrative multi-medium [...]" (Al Difraoui, 2012, p. 65) that did not only offer common news content, but also referred its viewers to their webpage and social networking activities. Its development and adaptation to online media also affected the outcomes of the Arab uprisings, especially in Egypt and Tunisia. Al Jazeera made use of the user generated content, constantly airing YouTube videos showing every facet of the uprising. Whether Tunisian or Egyptian national television, Al-Jazeera was accused of spreading falsified information in cooperation with the United States and Israel (Anas, 2012, p. 121), also denying the existence of upheavals on the streets. Whatever opinion people, governments or state media have about Al-Jazeera, the channel made a lasting impact on the general public by depicting people's call for democracy and provoking political and social change.

In 2005, Hugh Miles argued that "[...] the impact of Al-Jazeera on the viewer is not automatically translated into the process of democratic change [...]“, however, it "[...] does not mean that the channel has no impact on the democratic process at all“ (2005, p.338). This view prevailed six years before the first uprising in Tunisia, judging the channel's past approaches in dealing with controversial and sometimes objective matters, like the Iraq and Afghanistan invasions. It showed the channel's increasing influence in forming the Arab public opinion, yet, also foreshadowing Al-Jazeera's potential to facilitate change. The channels development onto multiple mediums made the people realize Al-Jazeera's role as a driving force for the protest (Tufekci & Wilson, 2012, p.365). In 2001, Kai Hafez characterized Al-Jazeera as "[…] a revolutionary force among Arab media […]" (2001, p. 331), also highlighting its immanent potential. Ten years later, Al-Jazeera showed how it could become the mouthpiece of a revolution. The current uprisings display an increasing trust among the people and their dependence on Al-Jazeera's fast dissemination of information. Tunisians increasingly relied on Al-Jazeera's daily reporting, being the only "[...] trustworthy local media“, that functioned as "[...] a mirror in which they saw themselves reflected“ (Hijjwai, 2011, pp. 68-69). However, Hijjwai concludes that Al-Jazeera is not responsible for the revolutions, it is merely "[...] a panel on the highway telling the revolutionaries: You are on the right path“ (2011, p.72).

Despite Al-Jazeera's controversial and often debated role, not only during the Arab Spring, but also ever since its establishment in 1996, it has gained major importance in the Arab region. Nevertheless, people have often doubted Al-Jazeera's subjectivity and condemned it as being biased and objective to the Arab cause (El-Nawawy and Iskandar, 2002, p. 22). News broadcasters generally follow the premise of neutral and unbiased reporting, however, the fewest actually succeed in doing so. El-Nawawy and Iskandar argue that "[t]here is a fine line between a real reporting bias and presenting the news from an Arab point of view to Arab viewers throughout the world" (2002, p. 52). News broadcasters have to decide whether they want to solely please certain influential individuals or speak up for the masses. Al-Jazeera has chosen the latter during the Arab uprisings and simultaneously succeeded in reinforcing the protester's call for democracy. El-Nawawy and Iskandar recognized Al-Jazeera's implied potential in affecting public opinion, calling for political mobilization and more profound debates among the people (2002, p. 55). Now, more then ever Al-Jazeera has taken on the role of "[...] challenging censorship imposed by the government-controlled media, addressing any relevant issue, [...] fundamentalism, state corruption, political inequality, and human rights violations" (2002, p. 206). Al-Jazeera's development, on technological and social level, has steadily transformed the channel from being a controversial, yet heard actor to an influential and empowering driver in the Middle East

7.3 UNDER-COVER BROADCASTING – *THE FUTURE OF JOURNALISM?*

As I have indicated throughout the paper, news outlets have increasingly relied on user-generated content as the primary source of information. Given the circumstances, being banned from on the ground news reporting, news agencies had to keep up and use the material that was existent. Relying on such content holds many dangers, as false reporting, due to unauthenticated sources may harm the credibility and subjectivity of the channels (Harkin et. al., 2012, p. 22). In order to obviate from such defaults, more and more journalists have discreetly found their way into the war zones. The Syrian government has been particularly strict and has banned every news agency from reporting from inside the country.

Al-Jazeera's' 'People and Power' series have aired a documentary called 'Syria: Songs of Defiance' about an undercover reporter, who had spent several months inside Syria, recording the events on the streets with his smartphone. Using a smartphone instead of a handheld camera gave him the freedom to move around without attracting great attention (Al-Jazeera, 2012). It also displays a possible direction journalism is heading to in the near future and the potential that lies in modern technology.

Another striking documentary has recently been broadcasted on the various platforms, showing Olly Lambert, an award-winning documentary filmmaker, being exposed to the dangers on Syrian grounds. The documentary shows the ongoing attacks at the Orontes River Valley in rural Hama. Lambert spent five weeks recording the events, witnessing the entire range of the conflict, both on the opposition and the government sides (Lambert, 2013).

8 Conclusion

Whether or not social media has the potential to change political landscapes is impossible to simply affirm or negate. It did certainly have an impact, since it has been increasingly used, yet, in how far remains to be seen in the future. Throughout the paper, various statistics (Dubai School of Government, 2011 & 2012) stood proof for the increased usage of social media in the affected Arab countries. The Internet and the social networking sites have definitely helped to disseminate information and to arouse the attention of the international community for the ongoing protests. The people in Tunisia and Egypt used these tools to facilitate change in public opinion and take governments by surprise. In the case of Syria, the government has rapidly adapted, in return exploiting such tools to their own advantage. The Syrian Electronic Army has restricted Internet activism, making it more dangerous for the parties concerned. The emergence of individual cyber activists was nevertheless crucial for spreading information and calling for protest.

In adapting to the changing media environment, Al-Jazeera as a traditional medium further accelerated the process of change. The cross-media convergence of online and offline media enabled the fast distribution of user-generated content for people to see in real-time. The interplay of both mediums describes the notion of the 'global village' (McLuhan, 1964), making it as relevant as ever.

In a nutshell, social media did have a certain impact, being a tool rather than a cause of the events of the Arab Spring. Moreover, Al-Jazeera's dissemination of the protests, regardless in what form, helped to facilitate the people's call for change. The people in Tunisia, Egypt and the rest of the World were informed either by social media or television broadcasters about the occurring unrests. However, the most astonishing fact is that people have overcome their collective fear that had been holding them back for decades. This newly acquired confidence was then transmitted to the public and eventually to the streets. To put it in the words of El Difraoui, "[...] there is no revolution without revolutionaries" (2011, p. 73). The people decide upon their fate, not technology.

REFERENCE LIST

Aday, S., **Farrell**, H., **Lynch**, M., **Sides**, J. and **Freelon**, D. (2012). *New Media And Conflict After The Arab Spring.* Retrieved 09/05/2013 from http://www.usip.org/files/resources/PW80.pdf

Al-Jazeera (2012). *Syria: Songs of Defiance.* Retrieved 22/05/2013 from http://www.aljazeera.com/programmes/peopleandpower/2012/03/2012 31213549186607.html

Al-Jazeera (2013). *Syria back online after internet blackout.* Retrieved 09/ 05/2013 from http://www.aljazeera.com/news/middleeast/2013/05/20 13581576 4712 12.html

Amnesty International (2010). *Syria: Detained female blogger at risk of torture.* Retrieved 22/05/2013 from http://www.amnesty.org.uk/news _details.asp?NewsID=19008

Amos, D. (2011). *Pro-Assad 'Army' Wages Cyberwar In Syria.* Retrieved 10/05/2013 from http://www.npr.org/2011/09/25/140746510/pro-assad -army-wages-cyberwar-in-syria

Anas, O. (2012). Facebook Campaigns in the Arab Uprisings. The Role of "Kulluna Khaled Said". In C. Schmidt (Ed.), *The Arab World: The Role of media in the Arab World's Transformation Process* (pp. 117-145). Bonn: Deutsche Welle.

Andersson, T. , & **Djeflat**, A. (2013). The Changing Landscape of the Middle East. In T. Andersson & A. Djeflat (eds.) *The Real Issues of the Middle East and the Arab Spring* (pp. 19-57). New York: Springer.

Arab Knowledge Report (2010/2011). *Preparing Future Generations for*

the Knowledge Society. Dubai: Al Ghurair Printing & Publishing House L.L.C. Retrieved from http://204.200.211.31/Update_ March _2012/AKR %202011/AKR_%20English.PDF

Asseburg, M. (2013). *Ziviler Protest, Aufstand, Bürgerkrieg und Zukun ftsaussichten [Civil Protest, Uprising, Civil War and Future Perspec tives]*. In Bundeszentrale für Politische Bildung, *Syrien [Syria]* (pp. 11-16). Bonn: Bundeszentrale für Politische Bildung.

Attasi, M. A. (2011). *What the people want...* In Al-Zubaidi, L., Khoury, D., Abu-Ayyash, A., Paul, J. *People's Power. The Arab World in Re volt* (pp.28-34). Beirut: Heinrich Böll Stiftung.

Awad, I. (2011). *Freedom is the Prerequisite for Bread.* In Al-Zubaidi, L., Khoury, D., Abu-Ayyash, A., Paul, J. *People's Power. The Arab World in Revolt* (pp.126 -129). Beirut: Heinrich Böll Stiftung.

Ayish, M. I. (2012). New Media in the Arab Spring Demystified! A Study of Satellite Television and Social Networks' Role in Arab Political Transitions. In C. Schmidt (Ed.), *The Arab World: The Role of media in the Arab World's Transformation Process* (pp. 97-114). Bonn: Deutsche Welle.

Aziz, M. (2013). *Syria Conflict to Harm Economy for Generations.* Re trieved 06/05/2013 from http://english.nuqudy.com/Levant/Syria_ Conflict _to_H-4621

Beckerman, G. (2007). *The New Arab Conversation.* Retrieved 03/05/2013 from http://www.cjr.org/feature/the_new_arab_conversation.php? page=2

Blight, G., **Pulham**, S. and **Torpey**, P. (2012). Arab Spring: an interactive timeline of Middle East protests. *The Guardian.* Retrieved April 19th, 2013, from http://www.guardian.co.uk/world/interactive/2011/mar/22/

middle-east-protest-interactive-timeline

Chozick, A. (2012, November 2012). For Syria's Rebel Movement, Skype Is a Useful and Increasingly Dangerous Tool. *The New York Times.* Retrieved 08/05/2013 from http://www.nytimes.com/2012/12/01/world/middleeast/syrian-rebels-turn-to-skype-for-communications.html?_r=0

Comninos, A. (2011). *Twitter revolutions and cyber crackdowns. User-generated content and social networking in the Arab spring and be yond.* Retrieved 14/03/2013 from http://www.apc.org/en/system/files/AlexComninos_MobileInternet.pdf

Delong-Bas, N. (2011). *The New Social Media and the Arab Spring.* In Oxford Islamic Studies. Retrieved 29/04/2013, from http://www.oxfordislamicstudies.com/Public/focus/essay0611_social_media.html

Deutsche Welle (2011). *The public face of protest in Egypt: Wael Ghonim.* DOI: http://dw.de/p/10F9j.

Dubai School of Government (2011a). Facebook Usage: Factors and Analysis. *Arab Social Media Report,* 1 (1), pp. 1-17. Retrieved 25/04/2013 from http://unpan1.un.org/intradoc/groups/public/documents/dsg/unpan044212.pdf

Dubai School of Government (2011b). The Impact of Facebook and Twit ter. *Arab Social Media Report,* 1 (2), pp. 1-23. Retrieved 02/05/2013 from http://www.dsg.ae/portals/0/ASMR2.pdf

Dubai School of Government (2012). Social Media in the Arab World: Influencing Societal and Cultural Change?. *Arab Social Media Report,* 2 (1), pp. 1-25. Retrieved 02/05/2013 from http://www.arabsocial me diareport.com/UserManagement/PDF/ASMR%204%20updated%2029%2008%2012.pdf

Eid, K. (2011). The Democratic Snowball And The Revolutions Of The Arab World. In Khalili, L., Schwedler, J., Zartmann, W. & Eid, K., *Revolution in the Arab World: The Long View* p19. Georgetown: Cen ter for Contemporary Arab Studies.

El Ahmad, K. (2013). *Facebook Users in the Arab World 2013.* Retrieved 22/05/2013 from http://visual.ly/facebook-users-arab-world-2013

El Difraoui, A. (2011). *Die Rolle der neuen Medien im Arabischen Früh ling [The Role of New Media in the Arab Spring].* Retrieved 28/04/ 2013 from http://www.bpb.de/internationales/afrika/arabischer-frueh ling/52420/die-rolle-der-neuen-medien?p=1

El Difraoui, A. (2012). The Web 2.0 Revolution and the Arab World. The Role of the New Media as Political Infrastructure: An Assessment. In C. Schmidt (Ed.), *The Arab World: The Role of media in the Arab World's Transformation Process* (pp. 61-87). Bonn: Deutsche Welle.

El-Nawawy, M. and **Iskandar**, A. (2002). *Al-Jazeera. How the Free Arab News Network Scooped the World and Changed the Middle East.* Cambridge: Perseus Books Group.

El Sharif, A. (2009). *Access to Online Information and Knowledge*. In Global Information Society Watch. Retrieved 30/04/2013 from http://www.giswatch.org/country-report/20/syria

Ferran, L. (2011, February 7). Egyptian Activist Known as 'Sandmonkey' Reveals Identity After Police Beating. *ABC News*. Retrieved 09/05/ 2013 from http://abcnews.go.com/Blotter/egyptian-activist-sandmon key-%20reveals-identity police beating/story?id=12853101#. UYvcb ZVDzl1

Fillion, R. M. (2013). *What You Need to Know About the Syrian Electronic Army.* Retrieved 14/05/2013 from http://blogs.wsj.com/corporate-intel

ligence/2013/04/30/what-you-need-to-know-about-the-syrian-electron ic-army/

Fitzpatrick, A. (2013). *How Skype Is Helping Topple a Dictator in Syria.* Retrieved 08/05/2013 from http://mashable.com/2013/02/04/syria-skype/

Fowler, S. (2013, April 25). Who is the Syrian Electronic Army?. *BBC.* Retrieved 11/05/2013 from http://www.bbc.co.uk/news/world-middle-east-22287326

Freedom House (2011). *Worst of the Worst 2011. The World's Most Repressive Societies.* Retrieved 20/05/2013 from http://www.freedom house.org/sites/default/files/WorstOfTheWorst2011.pdf

Freedom House (2013). *Syria.* Retrieved 25/05/2013 from http://www. freedomhouse.org/ country/syria

Gee, T. (2011). *Counterpower. Making Change Happen.* Oxford: New Internationalist Publications Ltd.

Gerhardt, W. (2008). *Prosumers: A New Growth Opportunity.* Retrieved 25/05/2013 from http://www.cisco.com/web/about/ac79/docs/wp/Pro sumer_VS2_POV_0404_FINAL.pdf

Gerlach, D. and **Metzger**, N. (2013). Männer, die auf Leichen starren [Men that stare at corpses]. Wie unser Bild vom Krieg in Syrien entsteht [How our picture of the War in Syria is formed]. In Aus Politik und Zeitgeschichte (APuZ 8/2013), Syrien. Bonn: Bundeszentrale für politische Bildung.

Ghannam, J. (2011). *Social Media in the Arab World: Leading up to the Uprisings of 2011.* Retrieved 04/05/2013 from http://cima.ned.org/ publications/social-media-arab-world-leading-uprisings-2011-0

Gharbia, S. B. (2011). *Digital Activism. Arabs Can Do It Themselves.* In Al-Zubaidi, L., Khoury, D., Abu-Ayyash, A., Paul, J. *People's Power. The Arab World in Revolt* (pp. 86-89). Beirut: Heinrich Böll Stiftung.

Ghonim, W. (2010). Breaking: Youtube Now in Arabic. Retrieved 08/05/2013 from http://arabcrunch.com/2010/09/breaking-youtube-now-in-arabic.html

Harkin, J., **Anderson**, K., **Morgan**, L. & **Smith**, B. (2012). *Deciphering User-generated Content in Transitional Societies. A Syria Coverage Case Study.* Retrieved 25/05/2013 from http://innovation.internews.org/sites/default/files/research/Internews_Syria_updated.pdf

Hijjwai, A. (2011). *The Role of Al-Jazeera (Arabic) in the Arab Revolts of 2011.* In Al-Zubaidi, L., Khoury, D., Abu-Ayyash, A., Paul, J. *People's Power. The Arab World in Revolt* (pp. 68-72). Beirut: Heinrich Böll Stiftung.

Hill, S. (2013). *Digital Revolutions. Activism in the Internet Age.* Oxford: New Internationalist Publications Ltd.

Howard, P. N., **Duffy**, A., **Freelon**, D., **Hussain**, M., **Mari**, W. and **Mazaid**, M. (2011). *Opening Closed Regimes. What Was the Role of Social Media During the Arab Spring?*. Retrieved 19/04/2013 from http://pitpi.org/wp-content/uploads/2013/02/2011_Howard-Duffy-Freelon-Hussain-Mari-Mazaid_pITPI.pdf

Hafez, K. (2001). The Role of Media in the Arab World's Transformation Process. In M. K. Hafez (Ed.), *Arab Media: Power and Weakness* (pp. 321-226). New York: Continuum.

Hofheinz, A. (2011). *The Arab Spring. Nextopia? Beyond Revolution 2.0.* Retrieved 07/05/2013 from http://ijoc.org/ojs/index.php/ijoc/article/viewfile/1186/629

Kassim, S. (2012). *Twitter Revolution: How the Arab Spring Was Helped By Social Media.* Retrieved 20/04/2013 from http://www.policymic.com/articles/10642/twitter-revolution-how-the-arab-spring-was-helped-by-social-media

Khoury, D. (2011). *Social Media and the Revolutions. How the Internet Revived the Arab Public Sphere and Digitalized Activism.* In Al-Zubaidi, L., Khoury, D., Abu-Ayyash, A., Paul, J. *People's Power. The Arab World in Revolt* (pp. 80-85). Beirut: Heinrich Böll Stiftung.

Krüger, T. (2011). *Das Neue verändert das Bestehende [The New changes the Existing]*. Retrieved 28/04/2013 from http://www.bpb.de/presse/51078/ revolutionsplattform-facebook-wie-das-internet-politische-umbrueche-beeinflusst

Lambert, O. (2013). *Syria: Across The Lines*. Retrieved 22/04/2013 from http://www.ollylambert.com/page5/page5.html

Landis, J. (2011). *Demonstrations in Damascus*. Retrieved 19/04/2013 from http://www.joshualandis.com/blog/?p=8410

Lehnen, E. (2011). *Slim Amamou – From Digital Activist to State Secretary*. In Al-Zubaidi, L., Khoury, D., Abu- Ayyash, A., Paul, J. *People's Power. The Arab World in Revolt* (pp. 90-94). Beirut: Heinrich Böll Stiftung.

Lynch, M. (2007). *Blogging the New Arab Public.* Retrieved 03/05/2013 from http://www.arabmediasociety.com/articles/downloads/20070312155027_AMS1_Marc_Lync h.pdf

Lynch, M. (2012a). *Political Science and the New Arab Public Sphere.* Retrieved 20/04/2013 from http://lynch.foreignpolicy.com/posts/2012/06/12/political_science _and_the_new_arab_public_sphere

Lynch, M. (2012b). *The Arab Uprising. The Unfinished Revolutions of the*

New Middle East. New York: Public Affairs.

Lynch, M. (2013). *Twitter Devolutions. How social media is hurting the Arab Spring.* Retrieved 30/04/2013 from http://www.foreignpolicy.com/articles/2013/02/07/twitter_devolutions_arab_spring_social_media?page=0,2

Malsin, J. (2013). *Portrait of an Activist: Razan Ghazzawi, the Syrian Blogger Turned Exile.* Retrieved 09/05/2013 from http://world.time.com/2013/04/02/portrait-of-an-activist-meet-razan-ghazzawi-the-syrian-blogger-turned-exile/

Matar, L. (2012). *The Socioeconomic Roots of the Syrian Uprising.* Retrieved 13/05/2013 from http://www.mei.nus.edu.sg/publications/mei-insights/the-socioeconomic-roots-of-the-syrian-uprising

McLuhan (1964). *Understanding Media. The extensions of Man.* London and New York: Bantam Books.

Miles, H. (2005). Al-Jazeera. How Arab TV News Challenged the World. London: Abacus.

Mohamadieh, K. (2011). *The Revolutions of the Arab Region. Socio-economic Questions at the Heart of Successful Ways Forward.* In Al-Zubaidi, L., Khoury, D., Abu-Ayyash, A., Paul, J. *People's Power. The Arab World in Revolt* (pp.112-118). Beirut: Heinrich Böll Stiftung.

Murphy, E. (2011). Between Image and Reality: New ICTs and the Arab Public Sphere. In M. Zweiri and E. Murphy (Eds.), *The New Arab Media. Technology, Image and Perception* (pp. 103-122). Reading: Ithaca Press.

Nazemroaya, M. D. (2011). *Is 1848 Repeating Itself in the Arab World?*. Retrieved 19/04/2013 from http://www.voltairenet.org/article168505 .html

Noll, A. (2011). *Revolution online. Das Internet und der Umbruch in der arabischen Welt [The Internet and the Transition in the Arab World]*. Retrieved 28/04/2013, from http://www.dradio.de/dlf/sendungen/ hintergrundpolitik/1488785/

Nordhausen, F., & **Schmid**, T. (2011). *Die arabische Revolution [The Arab Revolution]. Demokratischer Aufbruch von Tunesien bis zum Golf [The Democratic Transition from Tunisia to the Gulf]*. Berlin: Ch. Links Verlag.

Now (2012). [Interview with Blogger Shakeeb al-Jabri]. *Now Media.* Retrieved 21/04/2013 from https://now.mmedia.me/lb/en/interviews/the _revolution_will_be_blogged

Oghia, M. J. and **Indelicato**, H. (2010). *Ruling the Arab Internet: An Analysis of Internet Ownership Trends of Six Arab Countries.* Retrieved 30/04/2013 from http://www.arabmediasociety.com/?article=779

Rabbani, M. (2011). *The Arab Revolts. Ten Tentative Observations*. In Al-Zubaidi, L., Khoury, D., Abu-Ayyash, A., Paul, J. *People's Power. The Arab World in Revolt* (pp. 10-13). Beirut: Heinrich Böll Stiftung.

Ryan, Y. (2011a, January 20). The tragic life of a street vendor. *Al-Jazeera.* Retrieved 25/05/2013 from http://www.aljazeera.com/indepth/features /2011/01/201111684242518839.html

Ryan, Y. (2011b, January 26). How Tunisia's revolution began. *Al-Jazeera.* Retrieved 19/04/2013 from http://www.aljazeera.com/indepth/features /2011/01/2011126121815985483.html

Ryan, Y. (2011c, October 21). Tunisian blogger becomes Nobel Prize nom inee. *Al- Jazeera.* Retrieved 09/05/2013 from http://www.aljazeera.com/indepth/features/2011/10/2011106222117687872.html

Saeed, S. (2011). New Media, Public Diplomacy and the 'War on Terror'. In M. Zweiri and E. Murphy (Eds.), *The New Arab Media. Technology, Image and Perception* (pp.47-68). Reading: Ithaca Press.

Schmidt, C. (2012). The Transformation Process: From State Controlled Media to Virtual Freedom of Expression?. In C. Schmidt (Ed.), *The Arab World: The Role of media in the Arab World's Transformation Process* (pp. 12-21). Bonn: Deutsche Welle.

Smith-Spark, L. and **Van Heerden**, D. (2013, April 25). What is the Syrian Electronic Army?. *CNN.* Retrieved 11/05/2013 from http://edition.cnn.com/2013/04/24/tech/syrian-electronic-army/index.html

Sreberny, A. (2012). New Media and the Middle East: Thinking Allowed. *International Institute Journal University of Michigan*, 1 (2), 2-5. DOI: http://hdl.handle.net/2027/spo.11645653.0001.202

Srinivasan, R. (2012). Taking power through technology in the Arab Spring. *Al-Jazeera.* Retrieved 02/05/2013 from http://www.aljazeera.com/indepth/opinion/2012/09/201291911534429 9848.html

The Arabic Network for Human Rights Information (2012). *Syria: Activist Mazen Darwish and others detained.* Retrieved 09/05/2013 from http://www.anhri.net/en/?p=6862.

The Guardian (2011). *Syrian police seal off city of Daraa after security forces kill five protestors.* Retrieved 19/03/2013 from http://www.guardian.co.uk/world/2011/mar/19/syria-police-seal-off-daraa-after-five-protesters-killed

The Wall Street Journal (2011). [Interview with Bashar Al-Assads, President of Syria]. *The Wall Street Journal Europe Edition.* Retrieved 19/04/2013 from http://online.wsj.com/article/SB10001424052748703833204576114712441122894.html

Tufekci, Z. and **Wilson**, C. (2012). *Social Media and the Decision to Participate in Political Protest: Observations From Tahrir Square.* Retrieved 25/05/2013 from http://www.academia.edu/2493339/ Social_ Media_and_the_Decision_to_Participate_in_Political_Protest_ Observations_From_Tahrir_Square

United Nations Development Programme (2011). Towards the Develop mental State in the Arab Region. *Arab Development Challenges Re port,* 1 (1), pp. 107-110. Retrieved 11/04/2013 from http://www.undp.org/content/undp/en/home/librarypage/hdr/arab-development-challenges-report-2011.html

Uysal, A. (2011). The New Frontier in International Politics: The Nature of al-Jazeera's Prime-time Broadcasting in Arabic and English. In M. Zweiri and E. Murphy (Eds.), *The New Arab Media. Technology, Im age and Perception* (pp. 1-18). Reading: Ithaca Press.

Wikstrom, C. (2011). Syria: 'A kingdom of silence'. *Al-Jazeera.* Retrieved 25/04/2013 from http://www.aljazeera.com/indepth/features/2011/02/2011291031215 62395.html

World Bank (2011). *Egypt Arab Republic.* Retrieved 22/05/2013 from http://data.worldbank.org/country/egypt-arab-republic

Internet Economics / Internetökonomie

edited by / hrsg. von Prof. Dr. Julia Maintz (Cologne Business School (CBS))

Elena Trost
Social Media Marketing in BRIC Countries
Examining case studies of BMW, adidas and NIVEA

The economic growth and increasing Internet access within BRIC (Brazil, Russia, India and China) is opening new opportunities for companies to reach wider audiences. This study examines these opportunities and assesses how global companies are capitalizing on these emerging markets; in particular the degree to which digital marketing and social CRM through social networks are being used. For the purposes of this analysis, three German brands are examined in detail: BMW, adidas and NIVEA.
The author shows that regular interaction with Internet users and monitoring of social networks can result in companies experiencing an uplift in both public perception and engagement. Another aspect addressed is the cultural variance that needs to be taken into account when planning social media activities. This study concludes that presently the full potential of social media has yet to be utilized within the BRIC countries, and that there is a unique opportunity to be realised by companies.
Bd. 6, 2013, 144 S., 19,90 €, br., ISBN 978-3-643-90264-1

Laura Neises
Social CRM in the airline industry: Engaging the digital natives

Social media has found its way into most businesses as a tool to push sales. Yet its potential to create long-term customer loyalty is not fully exploited. Especially in industries characterized by fierce competition customer loyalty is key for sustainable success. But how can companies attract the future consumers? Born in the digital age, digital natives are powerful experts of social media and will dominate businesses. Building on insights from the aviation industry, this book develops an approach to use social media in a way that engages the digital natives in long-term relationships.
Bd. 7, 2013, 112 S., 17,90 €, br., ISBN 978-3-643-90397-6

LIT Verlag Berlin – Münster – Wien – Zürich – London

Auslieferung Deutschland / Österreich / Schweiz: siehe Impressumsseite